NEW YEAR, NEW ME

A GUIDE TO BECOMING YOUR BEST SELF

52 Quotes
for Every Week of the Year

@TMSCCSMOTIVATION & Paul Mavi Jr.

Copyright © 2024 by @TMSCCSMOTIVATION & Paul Mavi Jr.
All Rights Reserved

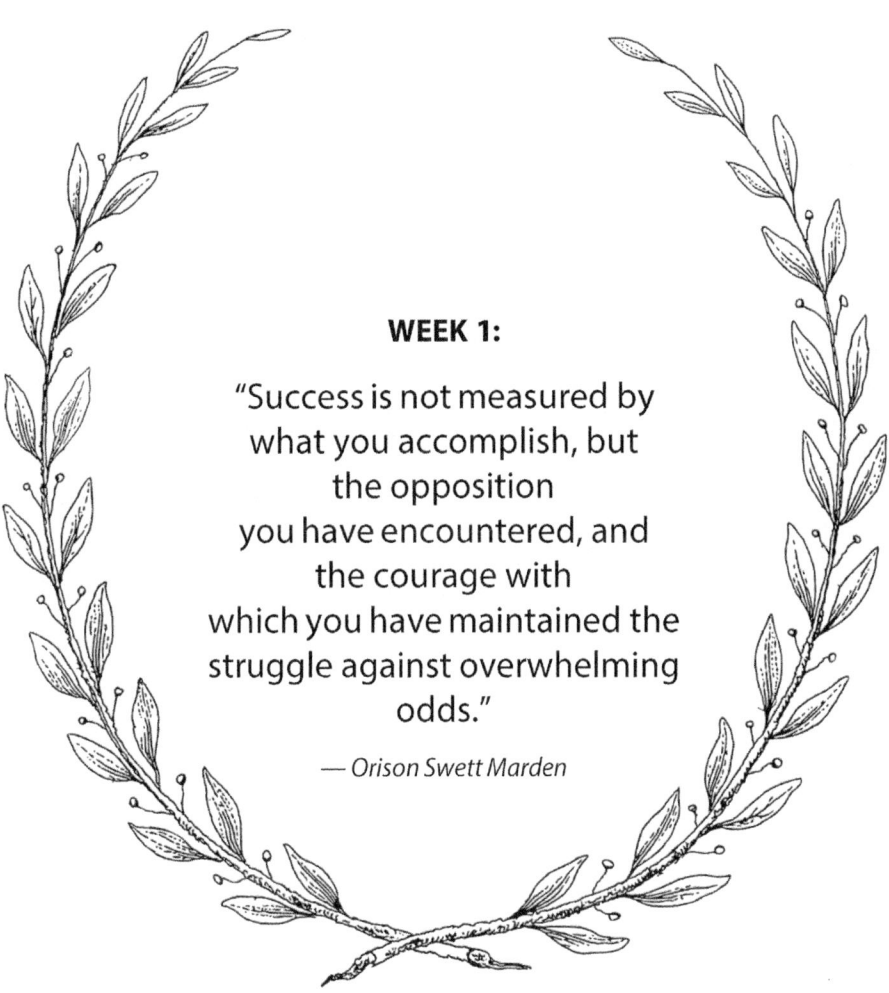

WEEK 1:

"Success is not measured by
what you accomplish, but
the opposition
you have encountered, and
the courage with
which you have maintained the
struggle against overwhelming
odds."

— *Orison Swett Marden*

WEEK 2:

"The only bad workout
is the one that didn't happen."

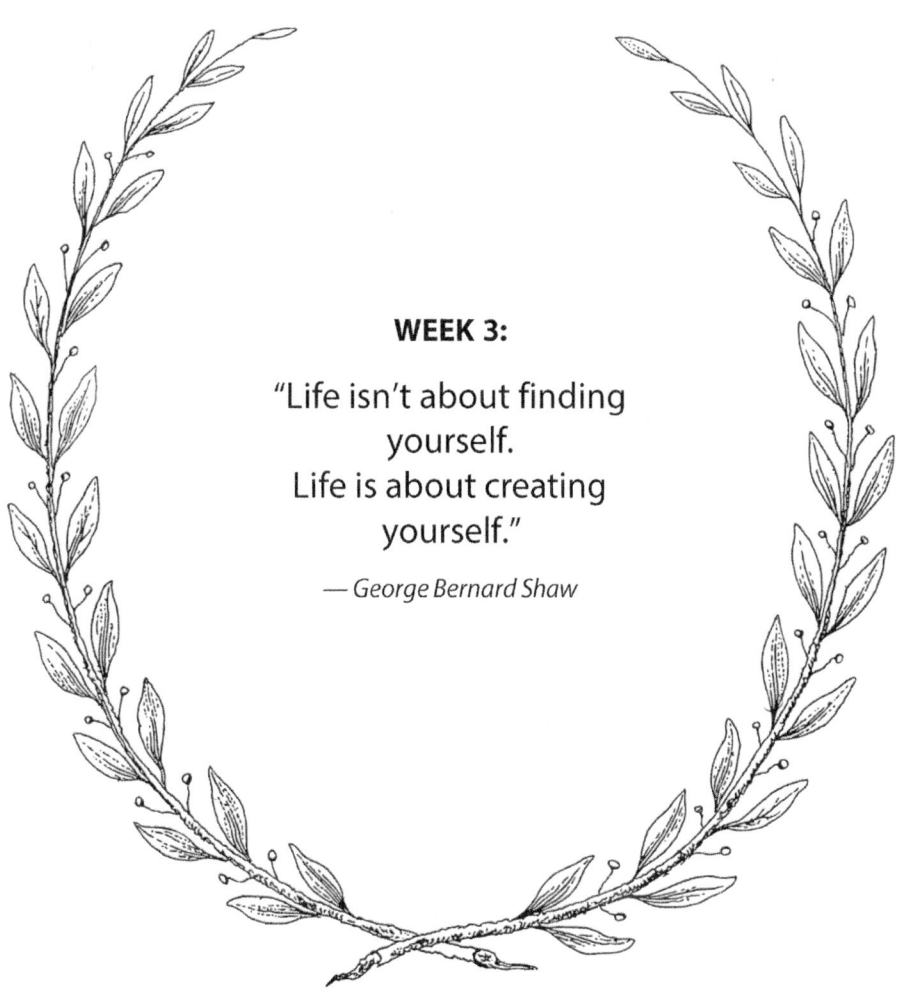

WEEK 3:

"Life isn't about finding yourself.
Life is about creating yourself."

— *George Bernard Shaw*

WEEK 4:

"In the midst of movement and chaos, keep stillness inside of you."

— *Deepak Chopra*

WEEK 5:

"The journey of a thousand miles begins with one step."

— *Lao Tzu*

WEEK 6:

"Happiness is not by chance, but by choice."

— *Jim Rohn*

WEEK 7:

"Success is walking
from failure
 to failure with
no loss of enthusiasm."

— *Winston Churchill*

WEEK 8:

"A quiet mind is
all you need.
All else will happen rightly, once
your mind is quiet."

— *Nisargadatta Maharaj*

WEEK 9:

"Live in the sunshine, swim the sea,
drink the wild air."

— *Ralph Waldo Emerson*

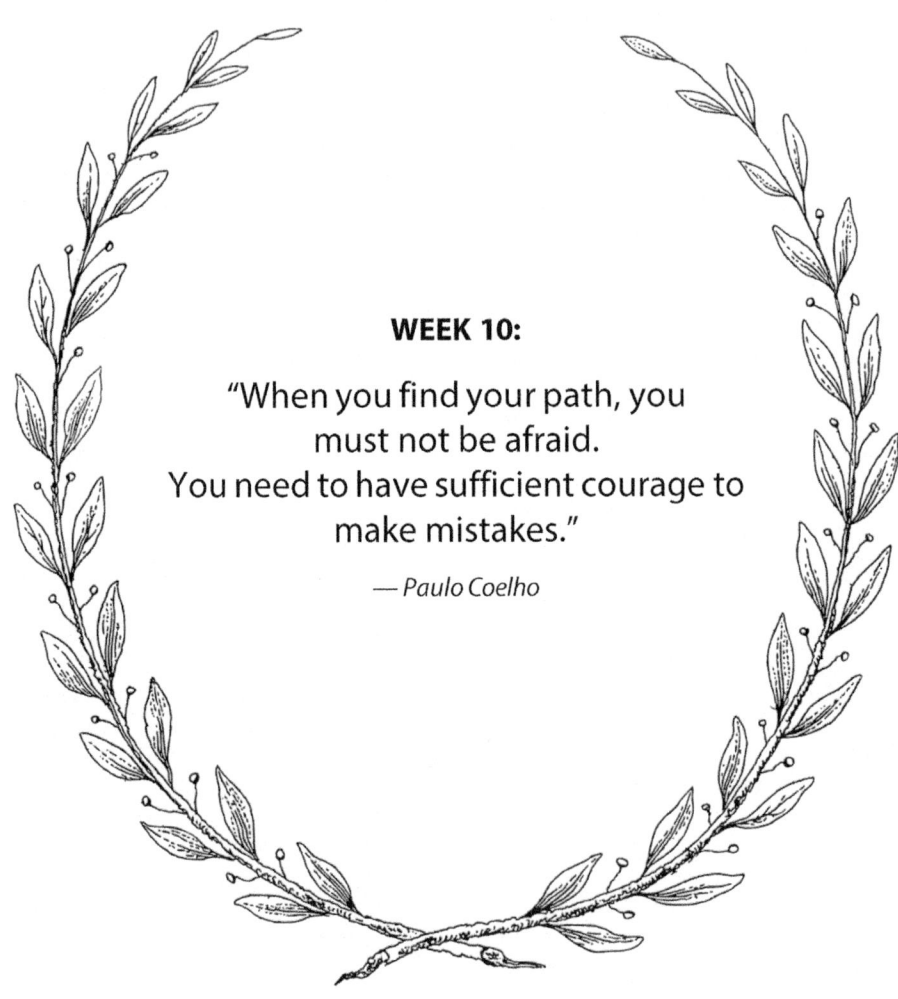

WEEK 10:

"When you find your path, you must not be afraid.
You need to have sufficient courage to make mistakes."

— *Paulo Coelho*

WEEK 11:

"The body achieves what
the mind believes."

WEEK 12:

"Invest in your health today
to enjoy the dividends tomorrow."

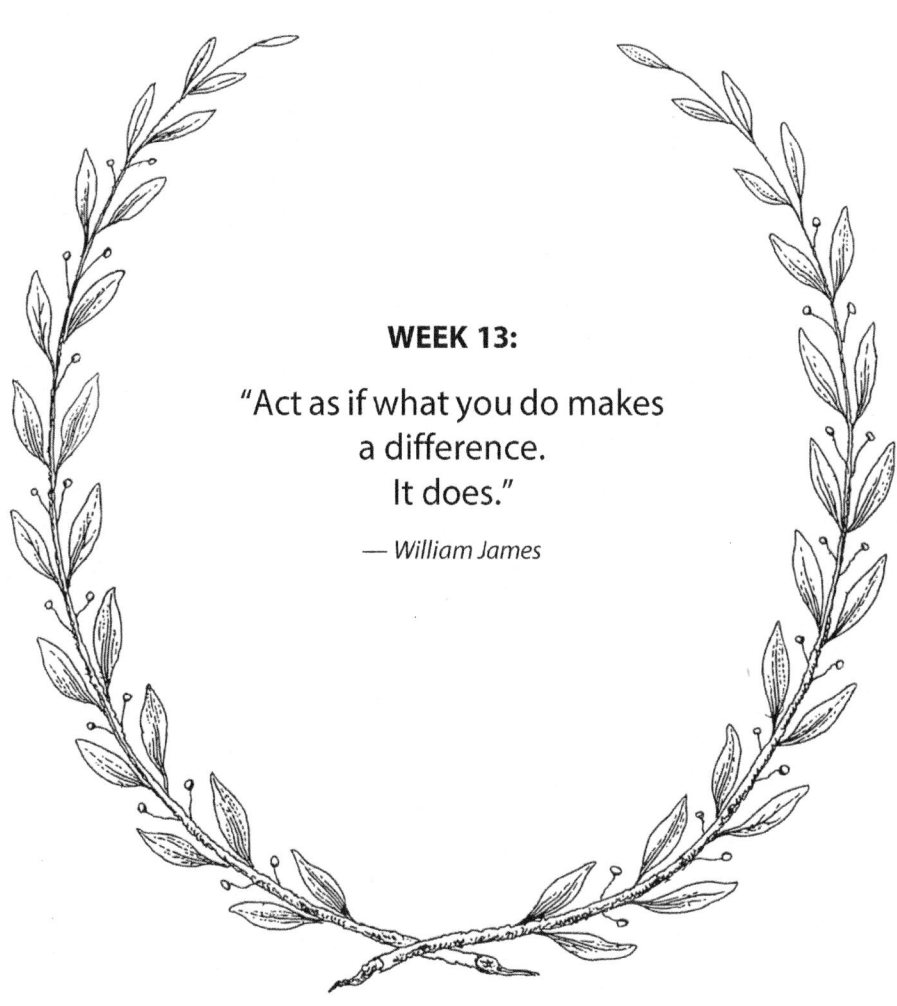

WEEK 13:

"Act as if what you do makes a difference.
It does."

— *William James*

WEEK 14:

"You don't have to be great
to start,
but you have to start to
be great."

— *Zig Ziglar*

WEEK 15:

"The only impossible journey is
the one you never begin."

— *Tony Robbins*

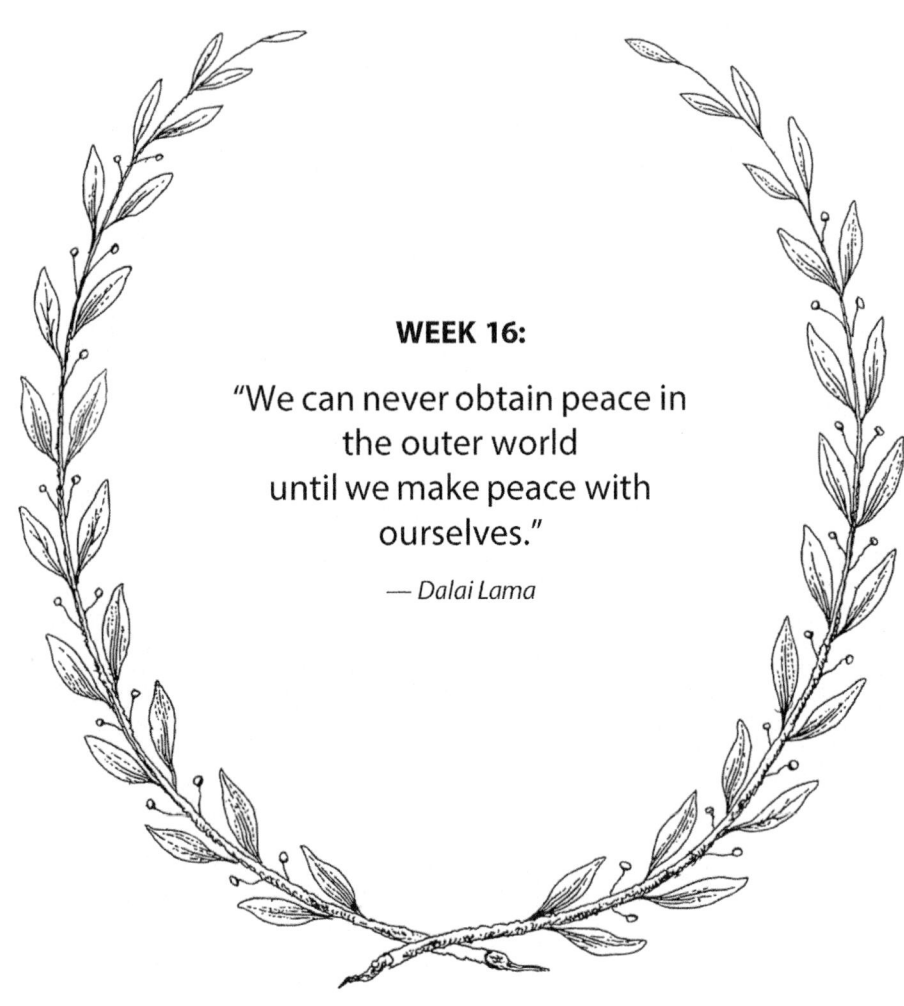

WEEK 16:

"We can never obtain peace in
the outer world
until we make peace with
ourselves."

— *Dalai Lama*

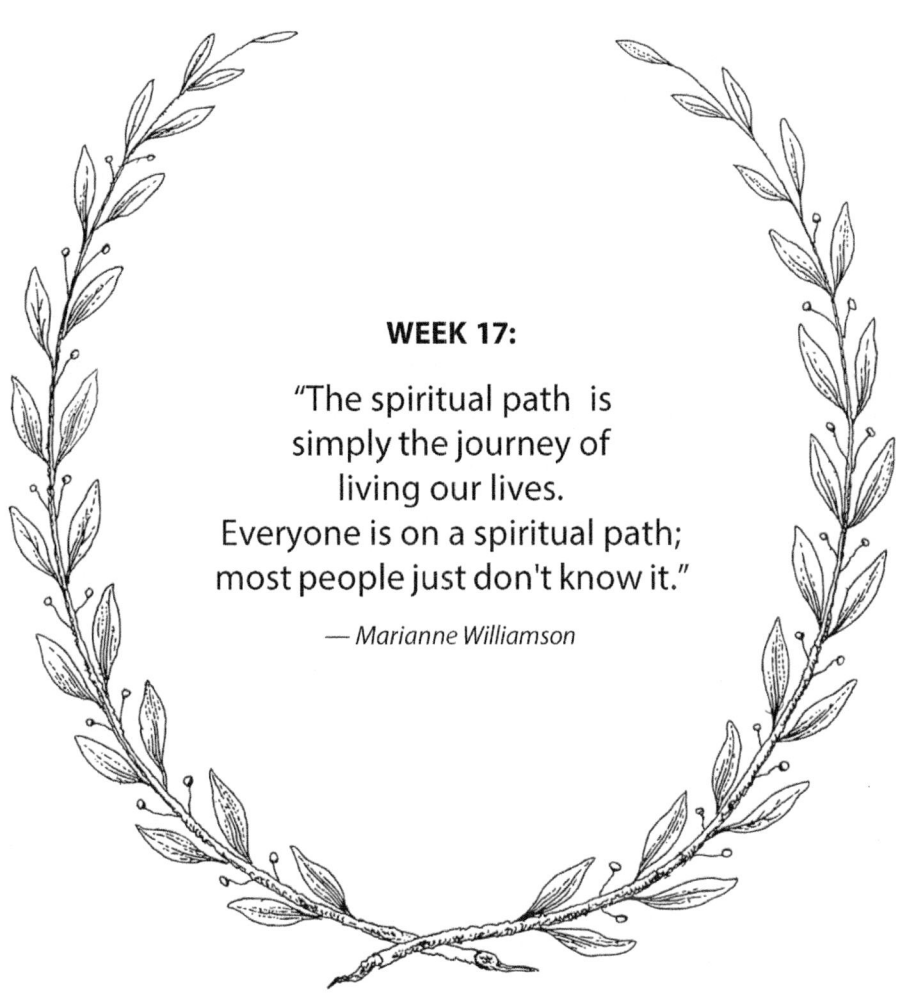

WEEK 17:

"The spiritual path is
simply the journey of
living our lives.
Everyone is on a spiritual path;
most people just don't know it."

— *Marianne Williamson*

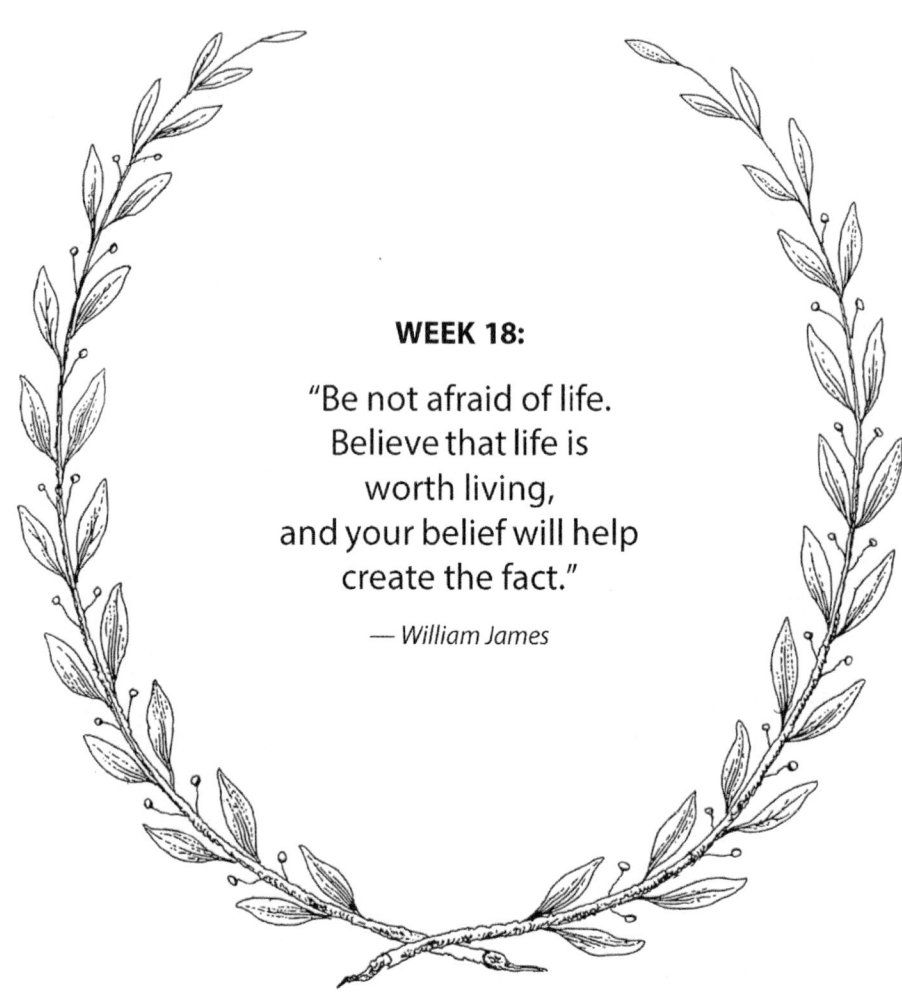

WEEK 18:

"Be not afraid of life.
Believe that life is
worth living,
and your belief will help
create the fact."

— *William James*

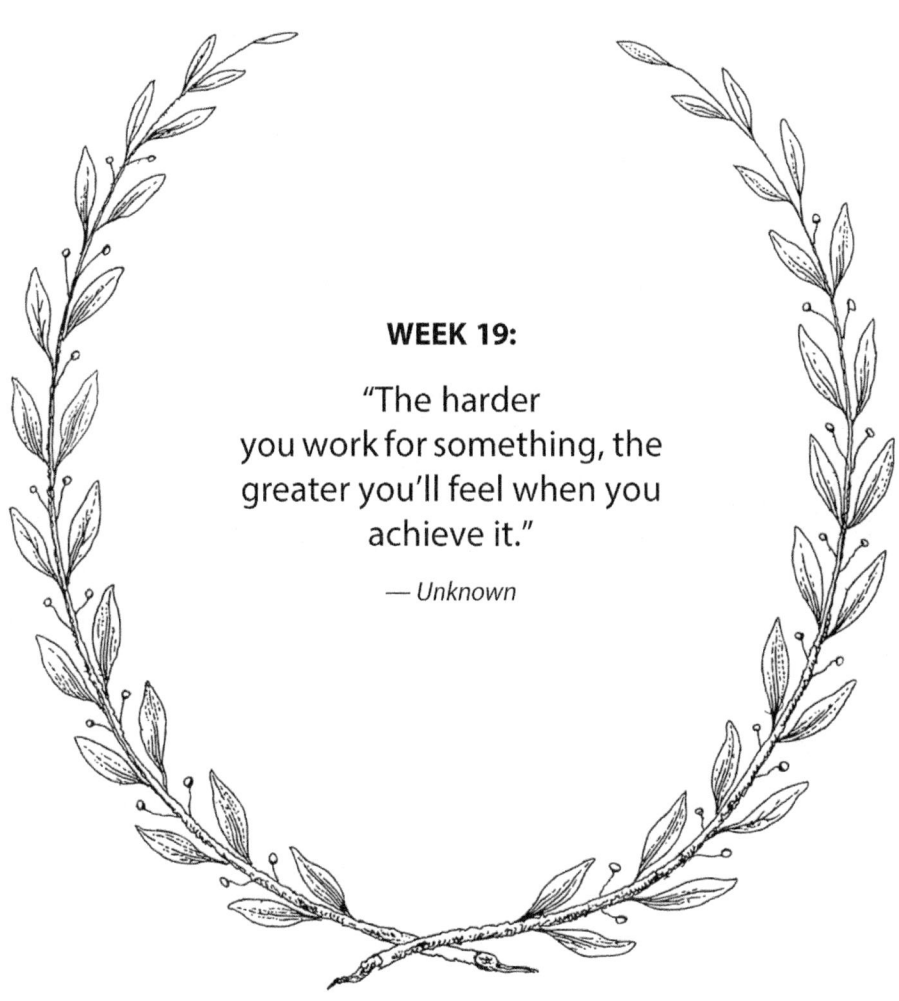

WEEK 19:

"The harder you work for something, the greater you'll feel when you achieve it."

— *Unknown*

WEEK 20:

"Your only limit is you."

WEEK 21:

"Your health is an investment, not an expense."

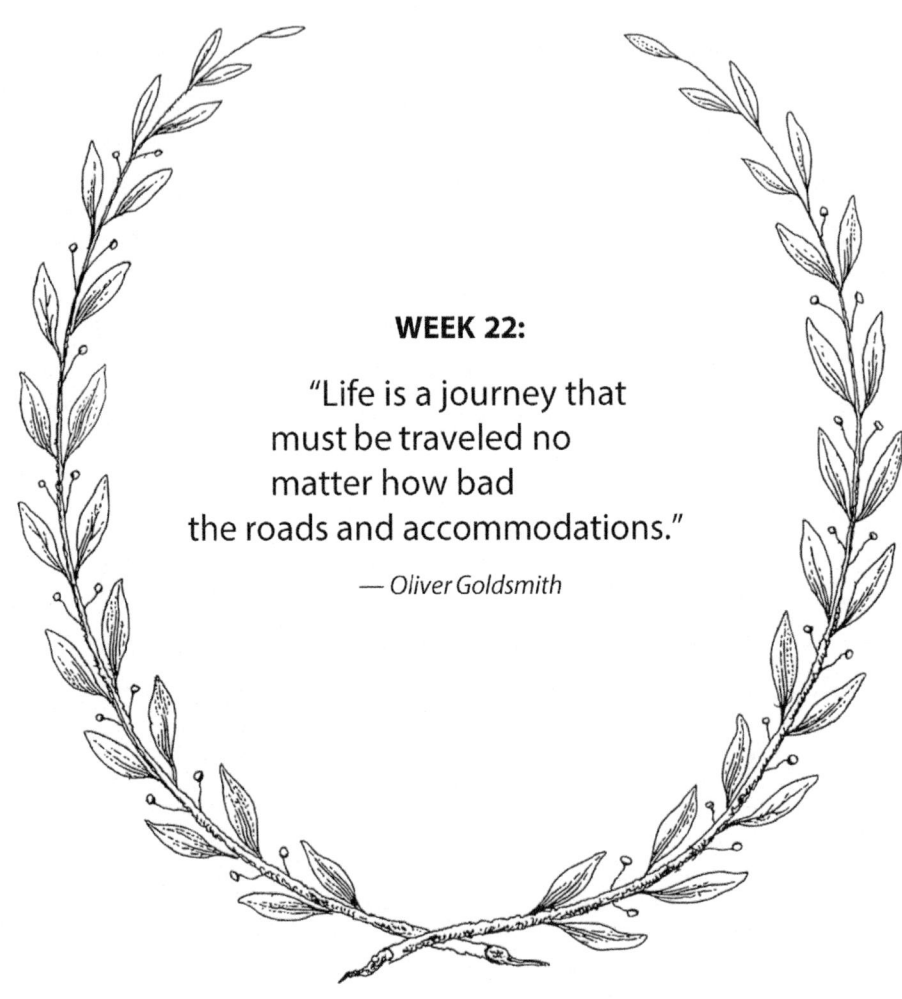

WEEK 22:

"Life is a journey that
must be traveled no
matter how bad
the roads and accommodations."

— *Oliver Goldsmith*

WEEK 23:

"The soul is placed in
the body
like a rough diamond,
and must be polished, or
the luster of it
will never appear."

— *Daniel Defoe*

WEEK 24:

"It always seems impossible
until it's done."

— *Nelson Mandela*

WEEK 25:

"Success usually comes to those who are too busy to be looking for it."

— *Henry David Thoreau*

WEEK 26:

"Fitness is not about being better than someone else. It's about being better than you used to be."

WEEK 27:

"Don't watch the clock; do what it does.
Keep going."

— *Sam Levenson*

WEEK 28:

"It does not do to dwell on dreams and forget to live."

— *J.K. Rowling*

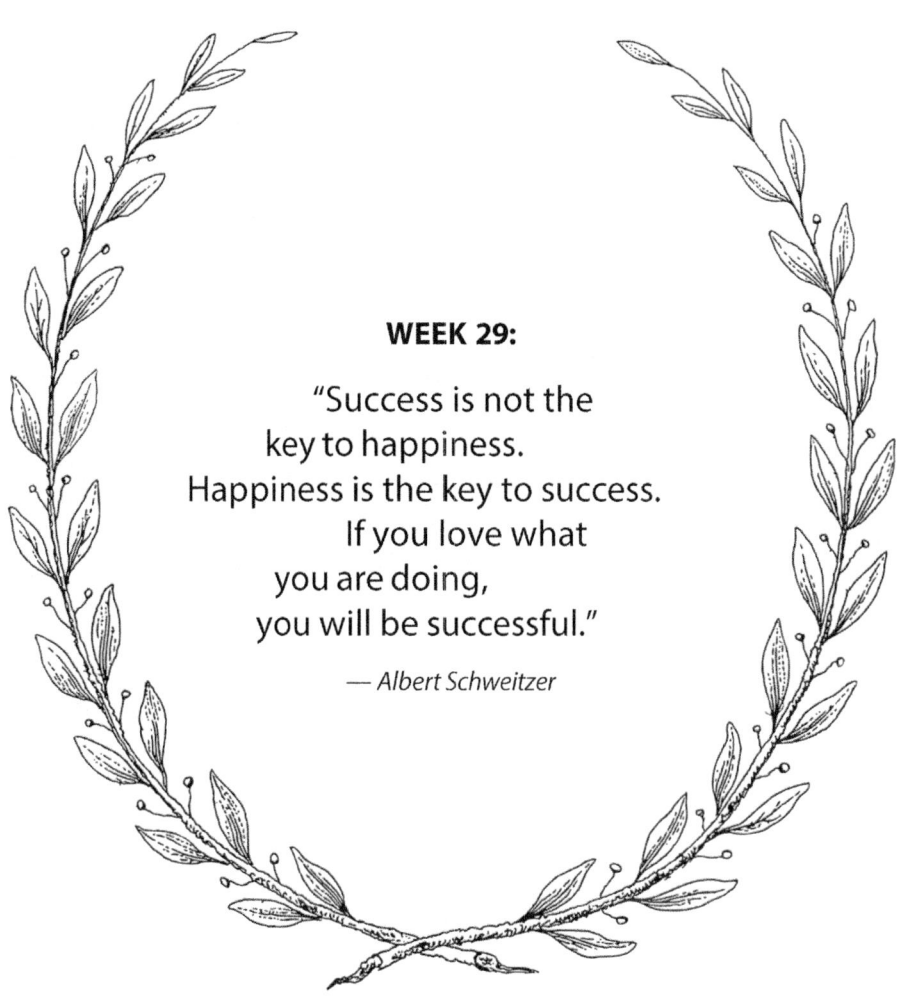

WEEK 29:

"Success is not the
key to happiness.
Happiness is the key to success.
If you love what
you are doing,
you will be successful."

— *Albert Schweitzer*

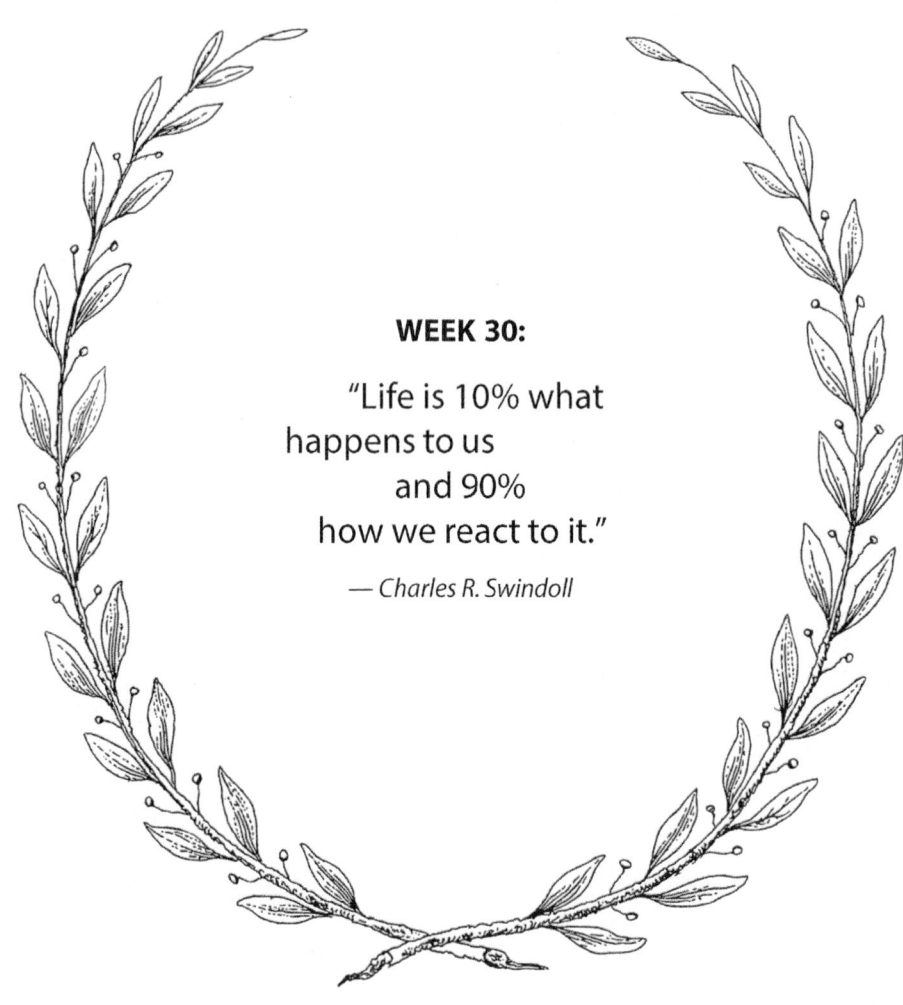

WEEK 30:

"Life is 10% what
happens to us
and 90%
how we react to it."

— *Charles R. Swindoll*

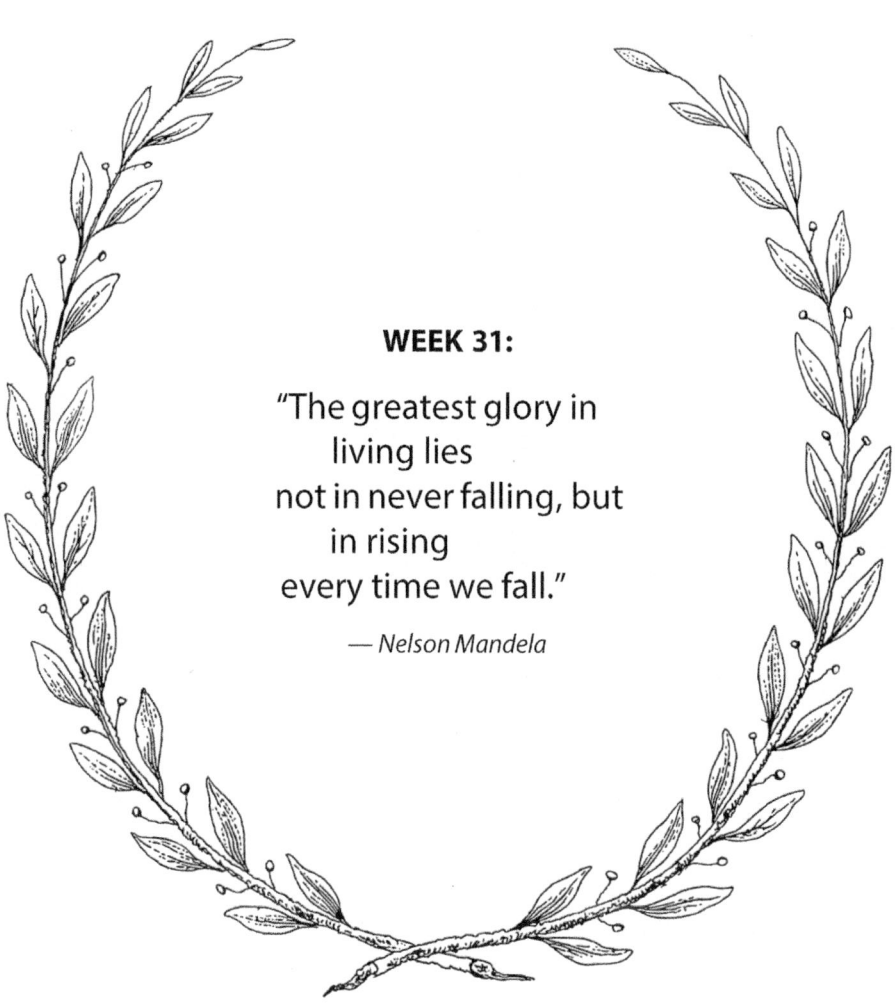

WEEK 31:

"The greatest glory in
living lies
not in never falling, but
in rising
every time we fall."

— *Nelson Mandela*

WEEK 32:

"Success is walking from
failure to failure
with no loss of enthusiasm."

— *Winston Churchill*

WEEK 33:

"The pain you feel today will be the strength you feel tomorrow."

WEEK 34:

"A year from now you
may wish
you had started today."

— *Karen Lamb*

WEEK 35:

"The best time to plant a tree was 20 years ago. The second best time is now."

— *Chinese Proverb*

WEEK 36:

"Inhale the future, exhale the past."

WEEK 37:

"Believe you can and you're halfway there."

— *Theodore Roosevelt*

WEEK 38:

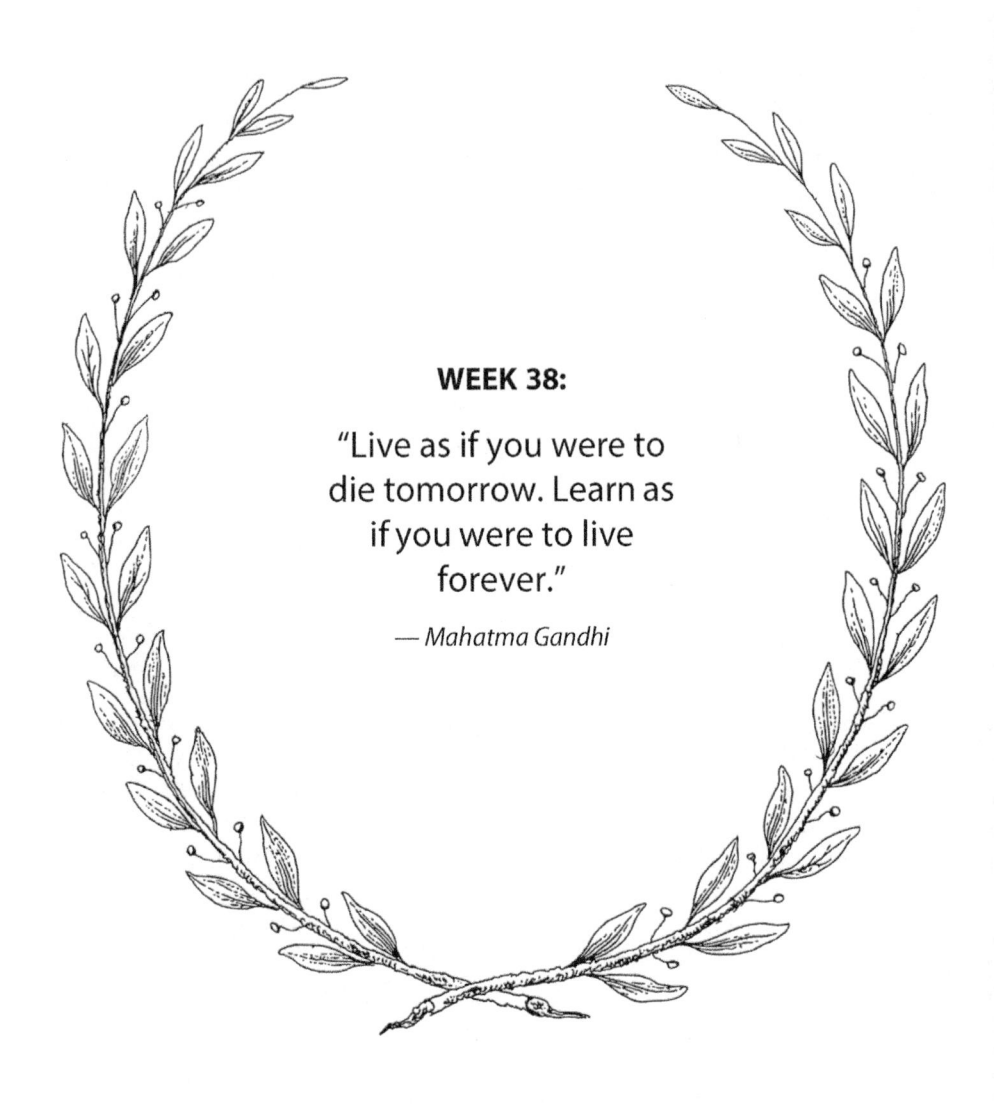

"Live as if you were to die tomorrow. Learn as if you were to live forever."

— *Mahatma Gandhi*

WEEK 39:

"The best way to get started is to quit talking
and begin doing."

— *Walt Disney*

WEEK 40:

"Hard work beats talent when talent doesn't work hard."

— *Tim Notke*

WEEK 41:

"God is in all men,
but all men are not in God; that
is why we suffer."

— *Ramakrishna*

WEEK 42:

"You are never too old to
set another goal
or to dream a new dream."

— *C.S. Lewis*

WEEK 43:

"The difference between a successful person and others is not a lack of strength, not a lack of knowledge, but rather a lack in will."

— *Vince Lombardi*

WEEK 44:

"Life is either
a daring adventure or
nothing at all."

— *Helen Keller*

WEEK 45:

"Every morning we
are born again.
What we do today is
what matters most."

— *Buddha*

WEEK 46:

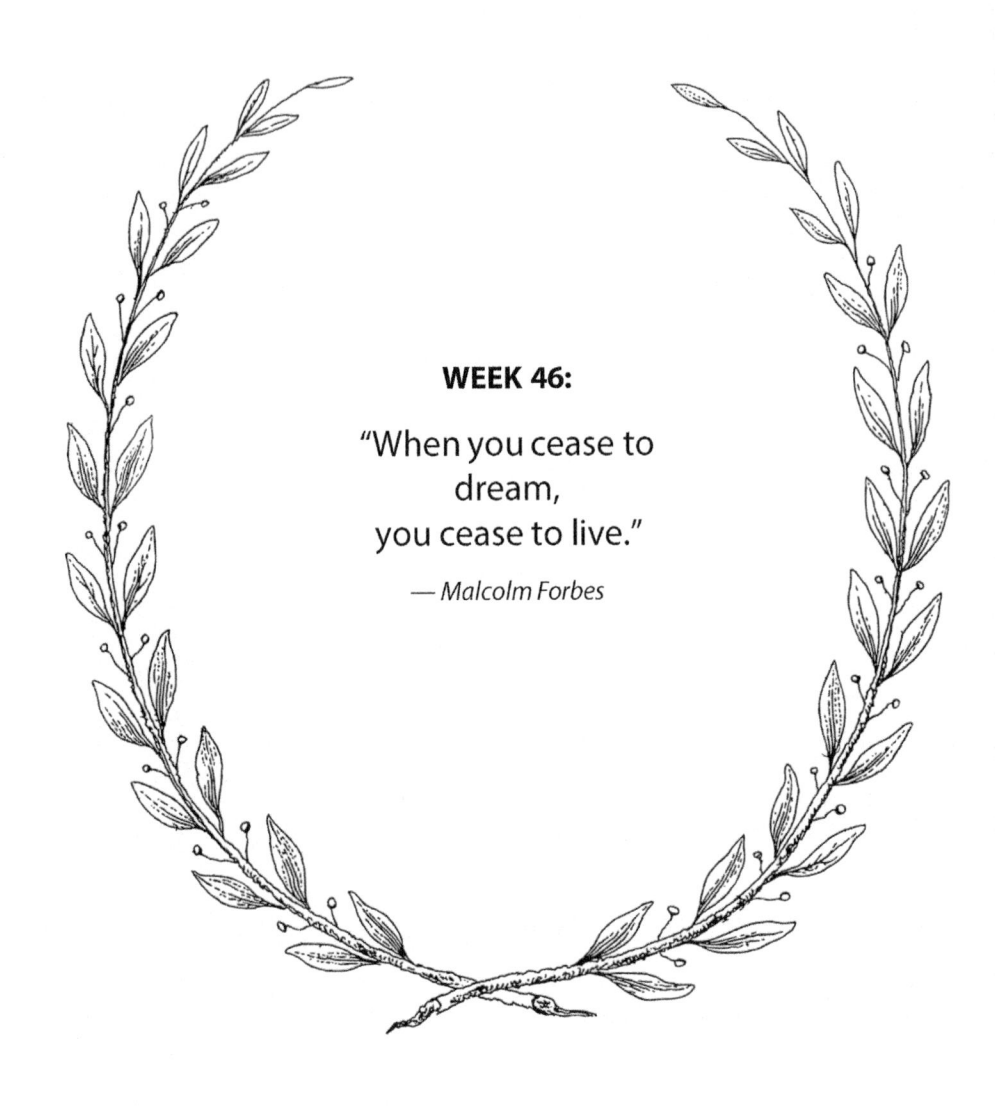

"When you cease to dream,
you cease to live."

— *Malcolm Forbes*

WEEK 47:

"Don't let the noise of others' opinions drown out your own inner voice."

— *Steve Jobs*

WEEK 48:

"Opportunities don't happen, you create them."

— *Chris Grosser*

WEEK 49:

"Believe in yourself and
all that you are.
Know that there is something
inside you that is greater than
any obstacle."

— *Christian D. Larson*

WEEK 50:

"Be stronger than your strongest excuse."

WEEK 51:

"You only live once, but if you do it right, once is enough."

— *Mae West*

Printed in Great Britain
by Amazon